TO : MAI
WITH LOT
FROM M

GOD BLESS YOU.

GW01398581

# The Damage of Murmuring to the Believer

*by*

## Gilbert M. Asare

**Grosvenor House
Publishing Limited**

This book is published by
Grosvenor House Publishing Ltd
28-30 High Street, Guildford, Surrey, GU1 3HY.
www.grosvenorhousepublishing.co.uk

A CIP record for this book
is available from the British Library

ISBN 978-1-907652-27-1

# CONTENTS

# About the Author

Pastor Gilbert Mprah Asare is the founder and head pastor of Crown of Glory Church, based in London with branches overseas. He is a very committed man of God, an anointed man of God, prepared for the end times by the Holy Spirit for the kingdom of God and takes joy in teaching God's word. He has been blessed with a dynamic gift of teaching; not only to the church, but also uses his gift efficiently as a professionally trained secondary school teacher. Teaching defines him as a person and to the Glory of God Pastor Gilbert Mprah Asare is a useful instrument in God's kingdom. Pastor Gilbert Mprah Asare holds BA (Hons) degree in Geography from the University of Ghana, Legon and PGCE from the University of London, UK.

His enthusiasm, in spreading the gospel, has led him to minister in various countries in Europe and other parts of the UK. Despite his busy schedule of ministering in the church and also teaching in the UK, he is able to fit in ministerial appointments in the UK and abroad. He is blessed with a beautiful wife, Evangelist Christiana Asare, an anointed preacher, who is also the assistant pastor of Crown of Glory Church. They have been blessed with four children; Gabrielle, Emmanuel, Stefan and Michaela.

# Foreword

This work is an excellent tool to educate the Church on the gift of foresight and its significance in the lives of God's people. The principles shared in this book will address misconceptions about murmuring.

**Pastor Martin & Katharina Meder**
**Church of the Living God.**
**New Jersey, New York**
**USA**

# ACKNOWLEDGEMENT TO GOD ALMIGHTY

In writing this book, I have had to rely on God the Father, God the Son and God the Holy Spirit for knowledge, understanding, guidance and power to complete it. I therefore want to express my gratitude to God Almighty for making the completion of this assignment possible. This work is an act of worship towards His name and I, whole heartedly, dedicate it to His glory. Philippians 4:13 "I can do all things through Christ who strengthens me".

## OTHER ACKNOWLEDGEMENTS

My sincere thanks go to the following people who have played tremendous roles in this work. To my wife Evangelist Christiana Asare; I say thank you for your spiritual, moral and physical support. Your counselling and encouragement has kept me going in challenging moments.

Rev Atsu Tettevi; for reading through, and making valuable contributions to this work.

Ms. Liza Georghiades; for your magnificent support. You helped to proof read the original work and offer useful contributions to the literary content. Your support has exceeded my expectation.

I also want to thank the congregation of Crown of Glory Church in the UK and Ghana for their prayers and encouragement. I am pleased to continue to serve as your senior pastor.

Now to my spiritual parents, Rev and Mrs Meder, I say thank you for your spiritual guidance, useful comments and support which were readily available to me when I called upon you.

To my earthly parents Opanin Samuel Baden Mprah and Mrs Susannah Lartebea Mprah, I say thank you for your love and the amount of effort and resources you invested in my life. The Almighty God gave you the vision and you responded positively to the challenge. I pray that the Lord's abundant grace be upon you and that you answer His call to salvation in Jesus name.

And to my children Gabrielle, Emmanuel, Stefan and Michaela, it is my firm belief that this will inspire you to offer yourselves as living sacrifices for the Lord and also to work hard in school.

To my brother and friend Mr Robert Appiah Kwarteng (aka NNBKK) your helpful comments and encouragement are priceless. May the Lord bless you and your family.

Finally, I want to make it clear, that I am fully responsible for the entire contents of this book. Unless otherwise stated, all scripture verses used in this book are from the King James Version of the Bible, which is also the New Open Bible Study Edition published by Thomas Nelson Inc.

# Recommendations

Pastor Asare has perceptibly and sensitively touched on, an undeniable failing in the church. This book is a timely reminder for the church and her leadership to address this embarrassment which is freely practised without restraint. Well Done. **Rev. Atsu Tettevi - Sovereign mission, London, UK.**

Pastor Asare, has chosen a subject which we are all guilty of – murmuring, to a greater or lesser degree. His book is a reminder of the murmuring Israelites and their demise as a result.

We all have our phantoms which haunt us from both past and present, but it is God's way, as Pastor Asare asserts of testing our loyalty, obedience and trust in Him. Instead of murmuring when faced with unsurmountable challenges, Pastor Asare, points us to what the real people of God did – pray humbly to God for strength and guidance to overcome all obstacles, using the challenges as stepping stones to strengthen our faith and ourselves.

Pastor Asare gives living examples of both murmuring people and those who trusted God, thus encouraging us to make the right choices, leading to inner peace. An inspiring read.

**Liza Georghiades, London, UK.**

The issue of murmuring as a result of fear is something every Christian who faces challenges along the way is bound to encounter and grapple with. How we react to this fear as individual Christians may be an indication of how much we trust our God. The hymn writer put it this way, "His (i.e. God's) love in time past, forbids me to think, that He will leave me at last, in trouble to sink" God has done so much for us as His people that it is unconscionable that we so easily forget, complain and murmur as well as doubt His ability to take care of us. This is why I feel so encouraged that the man of God has broken down this dangerous pitfall in simple layman's language to equip us as Christians to counter this devil trap of murmuring. Rev Asare's approach is original, practical and down to earth. It truly reflects a level of teaching indicative of God's Divine anointing. I highly recommend this practical book without any hesitation because I know you will be blessed. Your Divine breakthrough may be hidden in its pages. God bless you.

**Mr Robert Appiah-Kwarteng (NNBKK)**
**Assemblies of God Church**
**Virginia, USA**

# INTRODUCTION

Murmuring simply means complaining, grumbling or dissatisfaction with what we already have, have been offered or are expecting to receive, or even sometimes about what we do not have (this is bizarre and yet it is true).

Murmuring is a nature of the human race and is therefore an everyday occurrence in our lives. People murmur about their jobs, finances, marriage partners, physical appearance, the forces of nature etc, etc, the list is endless.

It would be wrong to suggest that this is a problem for unbelievers only. For it is a problem that affects everyone including believers in Christ Jesus, in fact ironically enough it appears believers in Christ are guiltier than unbelievers.

Some if not most believers do murmur about what happens to them in their faith life.

This book is going to explain why some believers do murmur, the damage that murmuring does to us, and how to stop it and receive our blessings instead.

If only believers in Christ could put into practice this verse of scripture, **'In everything give thanks; for this is the will of God in Christ Jesus concerning you'** (**1 Thessalonians5:18**), murmuring and its knock on evil effects would be snuffed out of the Church. Let us not forget that 'Faithful is he that calleth you, who also will do it' (1 Thessalonians 5:24).

I would at this point like to caution that murmuring is not a problem for new converts to the faith only (that is believers, people would describe as being young and immature in the faith). It is a snare to every believer; mature or immature believer, apostle or fledgling, the spiritual or carnal believer. In 1 Kings 19: 1–18, Elijah was murmuring about what he was going through in his prophetic ministry to the point that he desired to die. This was after his great victory over Baal's prophets on Mount Carmel. When Jezebel threatened to kill him, he fled for his life, sat under a juniper tree and said he had had enough and that God should take away his life. Now think about it Elijah the great man of God wanted to die because he felt he had had enough (**MURMURING**). How many great men of God have felt the same way at some point in their ministry? And even proceeded to make premature decisions. How many times have you heard a 'mature' believer say they have had enough? Have you ever said or are about to say you have had enough? Please don't say it until you have allowed the Holy Spirit to lead you through this book.

It is my fervent prayer that any believer that reads this book and is in the bondage of murmuring would be set free, and if you are not in this bondage, that God will strengthen you by His Spirit to enable you to resist the enticement to press this self-destruct button. God bless you.

# Chapter One

# Why Do Believers Murmur?

The fourth book of Moses, the book of Numbers is also called the book of Murmurings, for it is full of murmurings; by God's people (Israel) against God, by God's people(Israel) against Moses, by Moses against the people (Israel), and by Moses even against God. This is not surprising as it is the book of the wanderings of Israel during which an eleven-day journey became a forty-year agony. It therefore became a journey of frustration, desperation, despair, aimlessness, suspicion, fear, anger and lack of faith. This is not the only book that catalogues Israel's murmurings and their consequences, soon after their escape from Egypt, the book of Exodus also shows an ungrateful people murmuring against God's servant, Moses, and against God himself. A lot of believers today find themselves trapped in this problem as their plans and hopes take a long time to mature or bear any fruit, because, like the Israelites of old, they are full of unbelief which in turn brings divine discipline upon themselves and also hinders God's blessing for them.

## PRAYERLESS LIFE

This is a severe cause of murmuring. One of the most powerful weapons of each believer is prayer. Having a strong prayerful life lifts one up from the doldrums of life, be it spiritual, physical, emotional or financial. This is because it makes us strongly connected to our Father in heaven, act according to His will and puts us very much in the driving seat of life. This prevents murmuring.

Our Lord Jesus was faced with many attacks and opposition from the Pharisees, Sadducees, high Priests and even ordinary people and yet he did not murmur but endured the cross with joy, 'Looking unto Jesus the author and finisher of our faith; who for the joy that was set before him endured the cross, despising the shame, and is set down at the right hand of the throne of God.'(Hebrews 12:2). Facing problems, disasters, criticisms and attacks should not lead you to a point of frustration or desperation. Unfortunately, many believers have surrendered in spiritual battles once their weapons of prayer have, often, been abandoned. Our Lord was prayerful at all times, hence his power and authority over every situation that he came across. In Gethsemane the night before His trial, humiliation and crucifixion He prayed according to the will of the Father and did not murmur about what was about to befall him (Matthew26:39). He was able to endure everything that was thrown at Him to the point that when the women of Jerusalem wailed for Him, Jesus turned towards them and said, Daughters of

Jerusalem, do not weep for Me, but weep for yourselves and for your children(Luke23:27–28). It was a great opportunity too for Him to murmur about what He was going through but He did not. Believers should turn their moments of attack, anxiety, pain and suffering into a time of spiritual edification activities.

The apostle Paul is another shining example of a prayerful believer who never murmured. In the defence of his apostolic credentials and appeal to the Corinthian church to hold on to their faith in Christ in 2Corinthians11:16–33, Paul lists his sufferings in his service for Christ. This could have been interpreted as a boast but nay this was in response to the ungodly behaviour of some people towards him. In short he was drawing their attention to the fact that despite the hardships he had been through for Christ he was still strong in the faith and would not murmur at their ungodly treatment of him. Paul's case for murmuring is even clearer when we look at 2Corinthians12:7–10 – 'And because of the surpassing greatness of the revelations, for this reason, to keep me from exalting myself, there was given me a thorn in the flesh, a messenger of Satan to buffet me – to keep me from exalting myself! Concerning this I entreated the Lord three times that it might depart from me. And He has said to me, "My grace is sufficient for you, for my power is perfected in weakness". Most gladly, therefore, I will rather boast about my weakness, that the power of Christ may dwell in me. Therefore I am well content with weaknesses, with insults, with distresses, with persecutions, with difficulties, for Christ's sake; for when I am weak, then I am strong'. What an amazing statement or declaration by a firm believer in and of our Lord and saviour Jesus Christ. Paul says that he is happy with weaknesses, insults, distresses, persecutions, and difficulties for Christ's sake; a perfect scenario which appears to be a perfect platform for murmuring, which Paul resists unlike a lot of believers.

A lot of believers have murmured and do continue to murmur against elders, deacons, pastors, the church and sometimes even God. When people do not get what they want in the kingdom (healing, prosperity, solution to marital problems, family problems, breakthrough etc.), often carnal desires, they murmur, backslide in the process and in many cases leave the faith – their salvation is then put at risk and this can be dangerous. What a pity, they don't seek the will of God in their lives through prayer. Paul could have said "upon all that I have done for the kingdom, is this my reward?" and then he could have thrown it all away. But thank God he didn't, all because he was prayerful. He is truly a shining example of why we should not murmur.

**INGRATITUDE**

Gratitude is when a person accepts what they have been given and is thankful for. Right from the beginning of creation God has given us human beings in general and believers in particular a lot to thank for. He created us in his own image, made us stewards of this earth, and has given each one of us abilities as He deems fit. For us believers, 'But God commendeth his love toward us, in that, while we were yet sinners, Christ died for us' - Romans 5:8. His Son, Jesus Christ. This is how blessed we are.

However believers often fail to appreciate how much God has done for them. They look at other people, believers and non-believers comparing themselves to them and in the process highlighting or magnifying the differences between themselves, considering those differences as 'weaknesses', 'disadvantages', 'lack of quality', or 'lack of abundance', as the Bible declares in Malachi 3:14 'Ye have said, It is vain to serve God: and what profit is it that we have kept his ordinance, and that we have walked mournfully before the LORD of hosts? And now we call the proud happy; yea, they that work wickedness are set up; yea, they that tempt God are even delivered'. Meanwhile they fail to recognise their own strengths and give praise to God for them. A friend of mine, who was amazed at a labourer's weed-clearing skills, later consoled himself by recognising the fact that it would be extremely difficult for the same labourer to concentrate, read and understand a very short paragraph from his physics textbook. This example (and I believe there are several others) has led me to appreciate the differences in knowledge, ability, skill, wisdom and blessings between people. If only believers realised these different situations and would acknowledge the differences in their gifts and blessings from God, they would appreciate and not murmur. The Apostle Paul wrote about the diversity of the Gifts in 1 Corinthians 12:4-11; in fact he declares '....But all these worketh that one and the selfsame Spirit, dividing to every man severally as he will'. 'In every thing give thanks: for this is the will of God in Christ Jesus concerning you' (1 Thessalonians 5:18). Additionally, Apostle Paul declares in Colossians 2:6–7 thus ' As you therefore have received Christ Jesus the Lord, so walk in Him, having been firmly rooted and now being built up in Him and established in your faith, just as you were instructed, and overflowing with gratitude'. If you are firmly rooted in the Lord Jesus, each passing day of your life will be full of gratitude to Him and you will not murmur. Learn to be grateful to God for who you are and what He has blessed you with.

## LACK OF FAITH IN GOD AND HIS PROMISES (UNBELIEF)

Murmuring is as a result of lack of faith in God and His promises. In Numbers 14:11 Israel's sheer lack of faith in God angered Him for He asked Moses 'How long will this people provoke me? And how long will they not believe in Me, despite all the signs which I have performed in their midst?' God asked Moses this question in the presence of the congregation when the Israelites were murmuring and weeping over the negative report that had been given by ten out of the twelve spies of the Promised Land. The people of Israel's actions were a clear indication that they did not have faith in God. This is because they had the following options to take.

1. Pray fervently to God for guidance and victory.
2. Allow Moses time to enquire of God for further instructions.
3. Allow Moses time to meet with the spies to discuss and analyse the report critically and come out with some ideas.
4. Walk by faith and not by sight – take Joshua and Caleb's report and reject that of the majority ten. Remember there were two different reports (including Joshua and Caleb's).
5. Trust in God that He is able to do it again and again by referring to the ten plagues on the Egyptians, the Red Sea crossing, the provision of manna and quail, water from the Rock in the middle of the desert etc, instead they murmured. How often have believers forgotten what God has done in their lives and instead murmur bitterly when their faith is challenged again? This is probably due to the fact that past achievements of God in our lives count for nothing when we are faced with fresh challenges. These attitudes of believers have had a huge negative impact on Church growth with negative knock-on effects on the effectiveness of the impact of the church in the world today.

## LACK OF TRUST AND CONFIDENCE IN GOD'S STEWARD

Believers often question the leadership of the steward that God has appointed to lead His people. The people of Israel constantly questioned the genuineness of Moses' leadership on many occasions: In Exodus5:21(When Pharaoh made their task more difficult because of Moses' intervention); Exodus14:10–11(Pharaoh's army approaching them at the Red Sea); Exodus 32:1(When they saw that Moses had delayed to come down from Mount Sinai where he was meeting God).

How often have believers lost patience, trust and confidence in God's appointed servant, declared him useless, powerless, anointless, visionless and clueless? As soon as this becomes the perception the people have of their chosen leader it blocks the flow of God's power in the church and their lives. This is then when they begin to murmur, take premature decisions with disastrous consequences, in the same manner as the Israelites (They made gods in the place of the living God – an attitude and practice which was highly abominable to God). They begin to put their trust and confidence in friends (some of whom may be unbelievers) and carnal institutions like social services, human counsellors, financial advisers and others. Not that there is anything wrong with these institutions in themselves, but do not put your trust in them because the word of God declares that 'cursed be the man who puts his trust in man'- Jeremiah17:5. The apostle Paul also warned us in Colossians2:8 'Beware lest any man spoil you through philosophy and vain deceit, after the tradition of men, after the rudiments of the world, and not after Christ'. Believers need the motivation and guidance of the Holy Spirit through the power of prayer and not a worldly approach.

## LACK OF PATIENCE

Yet another cause of murmuring is lack of patience on the part of believers. A lot of believers have become 'fast food' answer seeking believers. They are always looking for quick fixes and quick results for their needs and problems. A lot of believers lack patience which is part of the fruit of the Spirit. In Exodus 32:1, the Israelites lost patience with God's servant, Moses, because he had not returned by their anticipated time. They therefore made an idol in the form of a molten calf and referred to it as their god who brought them out of the land of Egypt – something which was more than an insult and a great abomination to the Almighty God. Believers are hungry for 'instant and hasty' success because they murmur a lot about being left behind in life. This is usually when they compare themselves with others; a very unwise action because it puts them under more pressure to succeed and they forget about God's work in their life in the past. The Israelites were impatient when Moses was in a deep encounter with God on their behalf and proceeded to make an 'instant and hasty' decision with disastrous consequences. Some people have lost their travel documents and passports because of hasty decisions; others are in unsuitable marriages, wrong jobs, wrong relationships etc because of lack of patience. They wanted quick results hence they made hasty decisions. In Proverbs28:22, the Lord warns 'He that hasteth to be rich hath an evil eye, and considereth not that poverty shall come upon him'.

## VAIN GLORY

Proverbs28:26 declares 'He that trusteth in his own heart is a fool: but whoso walketh wisely, he shall be delivered'.

Philippians2:3 declares 'Let nothing be done through strife or vain glory; but in lowliness of mind let each esteem other better than themselves'.

Galatians5:26 declares 'Let us not be desirous of vain glory, provoking one another, envying one another'.

The scriptures clearly warn us about vain glory. Yet many believers have become willing victims of it. Willing victims because most of those who are trapped in this act do so deliberately (in other words they know what they are doing).

Some people enter the church with their own grandiose agenda. They enter the church or a ministry with the principal aim of securing for themselves a position of authority or influence, for example, to be a pastor, elder, deacon, deaconess, worship leader etc as if to say that it is only when you play a key role in the church that you would go to heaven.

When people with this mentality enter the church and do not achieve their hearts' desire, they become frustrated, rebellious and disruptive elements in the church. More often than not they leave the church making outrageous and hurtful allegations against the pastor and sections of the congregation with the aim of scattering the sheep. Their selfish and vain glory aims of their ego have not been met. They murmur a lot about the church, try to create distasteful scenarios in order to bring confusion in the church when they realise that they have been exposed and that their vain glory plans will not succeed. Such people wrongly believe that they have leadership qualities, they are better than many people in the performance of roles in the church. Sometimes, they even think that they are better than the servant of God appointed to shepherd the congregation. They then try to assume the position or role of an 'alternative' leader in the church. Such people always contradict, criticise or antagonise the work and effort of the leader(s) of the church and pour scorn on him (them). They are never humble nor sober, they are full of 'I can do it better than anybody else' spirit and they always murmur about everything in the House of God.

## DULLNESS OF HEARING

Dullness of hearing, which is the inability of the believer to receive or interpret messages from God breeds immaturity in believers, and this, can lead to murmuring. Lack of hearing leads to lack of discernment of the will of God in our lives. In such a situation every event in our life is misinterpreted by us; tests and trials become failures and then murmuring sets in. The word of God declares in Hebrews 5:12–14, 'For when for the time ye ought to be teachers, ye have need that one teach you again which be the first principles of the oracles of God; and are become such as have need of milk, and not of strong meat. For every one that useth milk is unskilful in the word of righteousness: for he is a babe. But strong meat belongeth to them that are of full age, even those who by reason of use have their senses exercised to discern both good and evil'. Believers whose spiritual hearing ability is impaired have serious spiritual growth problems which include; misinterpreting and misunderstanding the will of God in their lives, being unable to endure trials, afflictions and temptations, being unable to interpret and accept sermons wholeheartedly, being unable to interpret prophecies, being unable to respond obediently to God's call in their lives. The absence of such spiritual growth in the believer can lead to them not identifying God's purpose in their lives hence missing their blessings for most part of their lives. The reaction that comes from such believers is to murmur about how that they have never experienced the favour of God in their life and that it is not worth giving their lives to Jesus. The problem is not about Jesus, it is rather about the believers' dullness of hearing.

## CHAPTER TWO

# WHAT ARE THE EFFECTS OF MURMURING?

When the believer murmurs against God it affects both their physical and spiritual life.

## LOSS OF VISION

Murmuring blindfolds believers and takes away their vision in life. In Numbers 14:3–4, the Israelites demonstrated their gross loss of vision when they murmured against Moses and Aaron after receiving the reports of the spies of the Promised Land. They complained why the Lord had brought them out of Egypt only to kill them in the wilderness. In Numbers 14:4 they said '…..Let us make a captain, and let us return into Egypt'. What a disastrous decision? A nation has been rescued from their long time oppressors by God with great and mighty acts, and heading towards their land of abundant freedom; and then have a complete change of heart in the course of their murmuring against God based on the report that they had received from the majority of the spies about the Promised Land. The seeming challenge of the presence of the giants, the sons of Anak in the Promised Land was amplified negatively out of proportion and thereby caused the Israelites to ignore the blessings in the land. They then gave up the vision of moving in, to possess the Promised Land as ordained by God. Murmuring caused them to lose the pursuit of their vision. They had forgotten about the miraculous acts of God in their favour in Egypt. They had despised the power of God's deliverance for them in their challenge to enter the Promised Land. Many believers after being saved by the blood of Jesus, when faced with difficulties and challenges in their life, murmur a lot and lose their vision about eternal life 'the promised land', and look back to their past life in 'Egypt' yearning to go back (backslide) just like the Israelites. If you find yourself in that situation seek God through prayer and His word. Never lose sight of your vision of eternal life 'the promised land' because of murmuring.

## REBELLION

Murmuring leads to rebellion against God. In Numbers 14:1–4; 9–11. Israel's murmuring about the challenge of the presence of the giants in the Promised Land led to their rebellion against the authority of God Almighty. In verse four the Israelites had rebelled against God to the point that they called for the appointment of a new captain (leader) and return to their slavery in Egypt. This means they were no longer prepared to serve under the leadership of Moses who was called by God to deliver them from their slavery. When Joshua and Caleb tried to intervene and draw their attention to the power of God to deliver the land into their hands and thereby fulfil His promise, they grew more rebellious and wanted to stone them. The glory of God appeared in the tabernacle and the LORD said unto Moses, how long will this people provoke me? And how long will they not believe in Me, for all the signs which I have shewed among them? God was clearly angry at their rebellion (the result of their murmuring) against His authority. Believers sometimes act like the Israelites. If they do not get what they want in their own time, they refuse to seek and enquire of the Lord to know the Lord's will in their life. They murmur a lot and in the process consciously or unconsciously rebel against the authority of God. For example they will deliberately absent themselves from church meetings as we are warned about in Hebrews 10:25, refuse to support the work of God with their substance, begin to involve themselves in faithless talk, and some may turn away from the faith altogether. Be on your guard do not fall into this danger, because you bring upon yourself, the anger of God, when you rebel against him as a result of your murmuring.

## LOSS OF BLESSINGS AND INHERITANCE

Murmuring takes away the believer's blessings and inheritance prepared for them. Israel's continued murmuring against God's plan for them angered God very much. As a result they paid a very heavy price for it when God declared in Numbers 14:12, 'I will smite them with the pestilence, and disinherit them, and will make of thee a greater nation and mightier than they'. The Israelites lost their right to the inheritance that God had prepared for them through the covenant that he made with the patriarch and their forefather Abraham. It was an inheritance waiting for them to be taken but their ingratitude which was expressed through murmuring, led to God refusing to grant it to them. Again in Numbers 14:30 the LORD said 'Doubtless ye shall not come into the land, concerning which I sware to make you dwell therein, save Caleb the son of Jephunneh, and Joshua the son of Nun'. So a believer who continuously murmurs about their circumstances should know that they are murmuring against God, and that takes away the blessings and inheritance that comes with their salvation. Instead of murmuring the believer should continuously seek the face of God through prayer, fasting, studying and applying the word of God diligently (walk in obedience) in their lives, and exercise great faith in the face of all difficulties and afflictions. This is what Caleb and Joshua did and as a result they were the only people who were members of the **Generation of the Exodus** who became part of the **Generation of the conquest of the land of Canaan,** of which Joshua became the leader after receiving the mantle of leadership from Moses. Believers should avoid murmuring in their lives and continue to trust in God, because 'Faithful is he that calleth you, who also will do it' (1 Thessalonians 5:24).

## RISK OF THE WRATH AND JUDGMENT OF GOD

Murmuring angers God and we risk the wrath and judgment of God upon us. In fact God pronounced a judgment on the Israelites as well as ensured the withdrawal of the blessings and inheritance from them at the same time, in Numbers 14:27-32 God said, 'How long.....shall I bear.....with this evil congregation, which murmur against me?......Your carcases shall fall in this wilderness;......Doubtless ye shall not come into the land, concerning which I sware to make you dwell therein, save Caleb the son of Jephunneh, and Joshua the son of Nun........But as for you, your carcasses, they shall fall in this wilderness'. God punished the whole of the generation of the exodus with the exception of those below the age of twenty-one years, and Joshua and Caleb who had displayed a great amount of faith in him in the face of tremendous opposition from the rest of Israel. For as the two of them continued to affirm their faith in the Lord and encouraged the congregation that the land was theirs for the taking they turned on them to stone them. Sometimes believers who display tremendous faith in the Lord in difficult, trying and testing times are shunned by their fellow believers whose faith has vanished into thin air. They are called names, ridiculed and declared unreasonable. One minister's testimony goes like this: Years ago the church that he was serving decided to acquire a place of worship. The Lord revealed to him a particular site which was in the middle of no man's land. He was vehemently opposed by every member of the congregation including the elders simply because in physical and real terms it did not make sense to any one. Why are we building our church in a place where there are no souls? Where are the souls going to come from? The man of God was confident of God's word to him and so he pursued this vision to the anger and disapproval of the rest of the congregation. Soon after the completion of the building, the government of that nation started developing the area and before they knew it they found themselves in the middle of a new town, hallelujah!!!!

In Numbers 14:36–37, we read that the ten men who brought the evil report and made the congregation to murmur against Moses were killed by the plague before the LORD. They had received God's judgment. When believers murmur against God they stand the risk of being disconnected from Jesus and the salvation he has brought to them. They will become spiritually dead not able to relate to the LORD the way they ought to. Their prayer life will be weak, their spiritual hearing will be impaired, and their spiritual vision will desert them. There will be a total disconnection from the LORD unless they repent and be restored.

## THE CONSEQUENCES OF MURMURING, DELIGHTS THE ENEMY

Murmuring and the consequences we face makes Satan and his agents (witches, wizards, dominion powers and wicked spirits of higher places) very happy. Numbers 14:11–16 declares '..How long will this people provoke me? And how long will it be ere they believe me, for all the signs which I have shewed among them? I will smite them with the pestilence, and disinherit them….. And Moses said unto the LORD, Then the Egyptians shall hear it….. And they will tell it to the inhabitants of this land: for they have heard that thou LORD art among this people….. Because the LORD was not able to bring this people into the land which he sware unto them, therefore he hath slain them in the wilderness.' As the LORD became angry and as He warned Moses that He will smite the Israelites for their murmuring, Moses pleaded with God to forgive them because if He killed them, all the enemies of Israel, that is the Egyptians and the other nations who have heard about the great things God had began with the Israelites would be happy and claim that because God was not able to fulfil His promise of bringing them to the land which He swore unto them, that is why He has killed them in the wilderness(with the exception of those under the age of twenty-one years, and Joshua and Caleb, Numbers 14:29). When we murmur in our faith life and the unpleasant consequences come upon us Satan and his agents rejoice, we ridicule ourselves before unbelievers and it discourages them from receiving Christ. This has the knock on negative effect on our own spiritual and overall growth as well as that of the Church and God's kingdom.

## WITHDRAWAL OF THE PRESENCE OF GOD

Murmuring leads to the withdrawal of the presence of God and His power from our lives. In Numbers 14: 39–45, Moses warned the Israelites that the LORD'S presence was not with them anymore because of their murmuring, which had eventually led them to sin against God. In Numbers 14:42, Moses warned 'Go not up, for the LORD is not among you; that ye be not smitten before your enemies.' The severe murmuring led to the death of the men that brought the bad report to the congregation. When they realized the seriousness of their behaviour they mourned not only about the loss of the men who had died but also about the possible loss of the Promised Land, but were not repentant. They decided to move early in the morning to proceed to the Promised Land to possess it. It was then that Moses gave them the warning about the withdrawal of God's presence and therefore His power from among them. He told them their enemies, the Amalekites and the Canaanites would defeat them if they made the attempt to possess the Promised Land. They did not listen to Moses and when they went they were defeated. Believers must learn to genuinely repent when they murmur and sin against God and not just rush through some ritualistic motions falsely believing that, that it is enough or take God for granted with statements like 'God understands', 'God is forgiving and slow to anger' etc., and yet, have a defiant heart. **We must repent with a broken and contrite heart when we sin against God through murmuring.**

A believer who is always murmuring against God will never see the glory or power of God at work in their life. Such a believer is likely to face defeat in many challenges no matter how little those challenges may seem. Such a believer will find themselves in a dry and fruitless life which is a clear sign that they are stuck in their own wilderness. This is because the Holy Spirit 'the gentleman' would have said goodbye to them long ago.

# CHAPTER THREE

# WHAT MUST WE DO
# TO STOP MURMURING?

Murmuring has a very damaging effect on a believer and the church as a whole. It is therefore very important the believer positions themselves strongly in the Lord so that they do not fall victims to this danger.

## PUT ON THE LORD'S STRENGTH

You need the Lord's strength to enable you to fight against murmuring. Ephesians 6:10–11 declares 'Be strong in the Lord, and in the power of his might. Put on the whole armour of God that ye may be able to stand against the wiles of the devil.

For we wrestle not against flesh and blood, but against principalities, against powers, against the rulers of the darkness of this world, against spiritual wickedness in high (places of authority) places'. Believers must be aware of the fact that the battle is more spiritual than physical, it is fought mostly in the spiritual realm with its manifestation in the physical realm and so believers must put on the Lord's strength in the form of faith, prayer, obedience to the word of God, service to the kingdom of God, walking in the truth of the Lord, living in righteousness in Christ Jesus, and with the spirit of perseverance. All these requirements are found in Ephesians 6: 13–18, and the more you live like this the greater your resistance to murmuring is likely to be.

Apostle Paul was able to use this weapon effectively to prevent himself from this danger. In 1Corinthians 1:8–10 he wrote 'For we would not, brethren, have you ignorant of our trouble which came to us in Asia, that we were pressed(burdened) out of measure, above strength, insomuch that we despaired even of life:

But we had the sentence of death in ourselves that we should not trust in ourselves, but in God which raiseth the dead:

**Who delivered us from so great a death, and doth deliver: in whom we trust that he will yet deliver us;'**

Paul and his companions' situation in Asia was so dangerous that at one point they almost gave up. But the beauty of Paul and his companions' strong faith is that in the face of their hardship they learnt to put their trust in the Lord and not in their own ability or wisdom. If they had put their faith in themselves they would have failed and then most likely murmured against the Lord. Instead they put on the strength of the Lord by their continued faith in the Lord's ability to deliver them out of their crisis. And their faith was not misplaced as they were not betrayed by God.

Believers must have faith to put on the Lord's strength to take them through difficult circumstances and not to murmur.

## LISTEN TO POSITIVE AND ENCOURAGING COUNSEL

The Lord's counsel is so indispensable and precious to the believer that they must depend on it if they are to stand any chance of not falling into the murmuring trap. Romans 10:17 'So then faith cometh by hearing, and hearing by the word of God.' The powerful word of God should be a constant source of inspiration and motivation to you. The word of God declares in Micah 7:8 'Rejoice not against me, O mine enemy: when I fall, I shall arise; when I sit in darkness, the Lord shall be light unto me'. The believer should be able to reject Satan's temptation to murmur against God in difficult times and hold onto their faith by reading and listening to positive and encouraging counselling which only comes from the word of God.

Seek counselling and listen to private or public testimonies by Holy Spirit filled believers (including pastors, elders, deacons, and ordinary church members) whose contribution to your faith life will be invaluable in your quest to live a murmuring-free life for Christ.

Above all there is no better counselling than that of the Holy Spirit for the believer. The Spirit of the Lord who lives within you will be speaking to you countless times urging you to be patient and not to murmur, and rather trust in the Lord, please listen to Him.

## BE FULL OF FAITH

Hebrews 11:1 defines faith as follows 'Now faith is the substance of things hoped for, the evidence of things not seen'. Examples of faith were demonstrated by Abel, Enoch, Noah and the patriarch Abraham. All of these early believers of the true God passed the faith test with distinction and they are shining examples for us to follow. We must live by faith, and act by faith. The believer has to be full of faith in order to defeat the forces of murmuring. Hebrews 11:6 declares that 'But without faith it is impossible to please him: for he that cometh to God must believe that he is, and that he is a rewarder of them that diligently seek him.' The believer who is always murmuring has no faith and therefore does not please God. Such a believer is most likely to live a life of defeat because their trust and confidence is not in God.

2 Corinthians 5:7 declares 'For we walk by faith, not by sight.' Walking by faith and not by sight prevents the believer from murmuring.

In Matthew 9:20–22 Christ said to the haemorrhaging woman '……Daughter, be of good comfort; thy faith hath made thee whole.' This woman who had been suffering from bleeding for over twelve years, when she saw Jesus said within herself '...If I may but touch the hem of his garment, I shall be whole.' Faith is the key to unlocking our victories and stops us from murmuring.

In the book of Acts 16:23–26 we read 'And when they had laid many stripes upon them, they cast them into prison, charging the jailor to keep them safely: Who, having received such a charge, thrust them into the inner prison, and made their feet fast in stocks. **And at midnight Paul and Silas prayed, and sang praises unto God: and the prisoners heard them. And suddenly there was a great earthquake, so that the foundations of the prison were shaken: and immediately all the doors were opened, and every one's hands were loosed'.** After their great evangelistic and miracle work on their missionary journey they were subjected to this faith-killing ordeal.

But even in the darkest of moments the faith of Paul and Silas was unstoppable. The temptation for murmuring was very high, instead they were inspired by the Holy Spirit to pray and sing to the glory of God for their ordeal. The result? The power of God was released in their favour. Their chains were broken, their jailor was terrified, the magistrates who were in charge of their imprisonment were terrified and were humiliated to come over to them to beg them to leave the city after their release. In our darkest of moments believers should worship God instead of murmuring and the power of God shall be released into our life.

## HAVE JOY, PATIENCE AND ENDURANCE

Be full of joy and patience in times of difficulties. The believer must also begin to see difficulties as challenges and also the opportunity to grow and excel in their faith. Avoid the **why me?** Syndrome. It is not an easy option to choose but James 1:1–4 declares '...My brethren, count it all joy when ye fall into divers temptations (various trials); Knowing this, that the trying of your faith worketh patience. But let patience have her perfect work, that ye may be perfect and entire, wanting nothing'. The believer must exercise a great amount of patience and endurance in times of trials, attacks and temptations so as not to murmur against God and sin. In Job 1:21–22, Job said 'Naked came I out of my mother's womb, and naked shall I return thither: the Lord gave, and the Lord hath taken away; blessed be the name of the Lord. In all this Job sinned not, nor charged God foolishly'. This is what Job said after being informed that he had lost his oxen, sheep, camels, children and most of his servants in Satan's first assault on him. This happened to Job considered by God as 'a perfect and an upright man, one that feareth God, and escheweth evil' (Job 1:8). As if this was not enough there was a second assault on him. He was again smote with sore boils from the sole of his foot unto his crown. It was so bad his wife asked him to curse God and die, an act of spiritual folly, and a trap that a lot of believers sometimes fall into. But Job's reply to his wife's murmuring was very profound; he asked 'What? Shall we receive good at the hand of God, and shall we not receive evil?'(Job 2:10). And the scripture says in all this did not Job sin with his lips. Job displayed tremendous amount of patience and endurance during his loss, a very tempting situation for him to murmur against God, especially considering his strong relationship with the Lord. He never thought God had let him down. Yet some believers who have faced situations nowhere near Job's have failed the 'patience and endurance' test countless times through murmuring because they had often wrongfully thought that their relationship with Christ has not been appreciated by Him, hence their 'attacks, trials or misfortune'. In the end Job was restored to an even better position than he was before his ordeal. Believers must cultivate the 'Job' attitude if we are not to ruin our own lives.

## FOLLOW THE EXAMPLES OF OTHER BELIEVERS

Remember the experiences of men and women of God who have lived their lives for Christ through and through. Such believers did not murmur but counted it as a privilege to suffer for the sake of Christ. Paul's experiences in 2 Corinthians 11:16–33 which showed his readiness and joy to suffer for the sake of the gospel of Christ without any murmuring and again in 2 Corinthians 12:7–10 where he was given a thorn in the flesh so that he would not be exalted above measure and yet preferred to gladly glory in his infirmities, that the power of Christ may rest upon him is an exemplary conduct of faith more than worth following. At the end of his ministry Paul was able to declare with hope in 2 Timothy 4:6–7 'For I am now ready to be offered........I have fought a good fight, I have finished my course, I have kept the faith:'

Believers must aim to make this statement by Paul their own when the time comes for them to begin their journey into eternity.

Also the early disciples rejoiced that they were counted worthy to suffer shame for the name of Christ, as they were beaten by the Sanhedrin in Acts 5: 40–41. There are many other examples: Hosea (suffering pain and contempt of living with an adulterous wife), Isaiah (persecuted for his uncompromising and sincere messages), Jeremiah (suffered for his radical message of God's judgment) and David (on the run as a fugitive from Saul), all went through extraordinary difficulties and challenges and yet they did not murmur. Believers must learn from these pioneers of the faith.

## COUNT YOUR BLESSINGS

Whenever you face any difficulties, hardships, problems, anxieties or dangers instead of murmuring about the situation in which you find yourself, begin to count your blessings that you have received from the Lord in the past. As you count your blessings by way of testimonies, God is glorified and Satan is defeated and put to shame. Counting your blessings received from God releases the power of God in your life for breakthroughs and miracles.

Whenever I face any challenges in my life I do not murmur, instead I begin to count my blessings in the Lord by way of testimonies. The Lord delivered me from the jaws of death in the heart of Sefwi forest late in the night in the western region of Ghana when the Lord intervened to stop a drunken man who had volunteered to carry my younger brother and me across a single-log and narrow bridge from dropping us into a deep river. The Lord opened the doors for me to come to Europe for a purpose when all seemed lost. In fact I arrived in Europe at midnight of the deadline date which had been set for me. The Lord has established my family and me in this nation in spite of all the different challenges that I have faced.

As you read this book I challenge you to begin to count your blessings in the LORD and you will be surprised about how far the good LORD has taken you.

# CHAPTER FOUR

# CONCLUSION: CONFESSION, REPENTANCE AND RESTORATION

It is a fact that a lot of believers both mature and immature have murmured in their Christian lives and have therefore paid heavy price for it.

I have heard a lot of believers murmur a lot; some have even foolishly declared that they are at loggerheads with God.

Some time ago in Ghana in the early 1980s a middle-aged man in a conversation with a friend of mine confessed that he had backslidden and had turned to idol worship because after following God for a long time he had gained nothing, apparently referring to his lack of material benefits. I later learnt that his daughter had been knocked down and killed by a car on the day of her engagement. His reaction might have been like this, what did I do to deserve this? Where was God when this was about to take place? Why didn't God spare me this ordeal? As a result of all these unanswered questions bitterness and murmuring set in, he made a premature decision and quit the faith. He is not the only classic example; there are many other examples within the body of Christ. Our strong desire to always secure our hearts desire which more often than not is outside the will of God for ourselves because they are carnally driven, often leads us to failures. We then turn on our God almighty and blame Him for those failures.

We have very much become solution seeking believers, somehow wrongly believing that the power of God is only expressed in how often He solves our problems or meets us at the point of our needs. Hence we find many so called believers chasing after miracles which become elusive to them and yet never grow tired of chasing after. They never settle down in a single church or ministry, instead they have become rolling stones or butterfly Christians shuffling through churches.

The time has come for us to say enough is enough to our immaturity and unfaithfulness, seriously seek the Lord and develop a meaningful relationship with Him and desire to worship Him in the beauty of His holiness. We can only do this when we say, Father thy will be done in our lives.

Dear reader if you have ever murmured against God like the Israelites of old, and other believers have done over the years, now is the time to repent, seek forgiveness and restoration for 'The Lord is merciful and gracious, slow to anger, and plenteous in mercy'(Psalm 103:8). Get on your knees and pray this prayer:

**Father God I confess that over the past years I have been a murmurer, I am truly sorry for all the**

unfaithful, ungrateful and insolent behaviour I have displayed towards you and your kingdom. I now declare my faith in your promises and will never go wayward again. Spirit of the Living God, please fall afresh on me; break me, melt me, mould me, fill me and use me in whatever way you want. I am yours now, and forever and ever. Amen.

The following verses from the Bible should be read and in some cases memorized to help and inspire believers when they are tempted to murmur because of any difficulties or challenges that they face.

Jeremiah 29:11 – For I know the thoughts that I think toward you, saith the LORD thoughts of peace, and not of evil, to give you an expected end.

Psalm 34: 7 – The angel of the Lord encampeth round about them that fear him, and delivereth them.

Psalm34:10 – The young lions do lack, and suffer hunger: but they that seek the LORD shall not want any good thing.

Psalm34:15 – The eyes of the LORD are upon the righteous, and his ears are open unto their cry.

Psalm34:19 – Many are the afflictions of the righteous: but the LORD delivereth him out of them all.

Psalm 37:1 – Fret not thyself because of evildoers, neither be thou envious against the workers of iniquity.

Psalm 37:25 – I have been young, and now am old; yet have I not seen the righteous forsaken, nor his seed begging bread.

Philippians4:11 – Not that I speak in respect of want: for I have learned, in whatsoever state I am, therewith to be content.

Philippians4:12 – I know both how to be abased, and I know how to abound: every where and in all things I am instructed both to be full and to be hungry, both to abound and to suffer need.

Philippians4:13 – I can do all things through Christ which strengtheneth me.

Brethren there are many other inspiring verses in the Bible that you will come across and find very useful as you diligently study it day by day.

May the awesome and almighty God continue to be your God even as you faithfully abide under His grace despite all the challenges that you are going through.